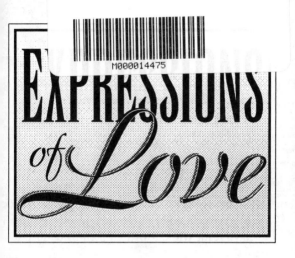

EXPRESSIONS of Love

by
Jerold C. Potter

A Barbour Book

Other Books by Jerold C. Potter
Books of the Bible
My Bible Study Notebook
How to Conquer Anger
How to Conquer Fear
How to Conquer Worry
How to Conquer Unforgiveness

© MCMXCVI by Barbour & Company, Inc.

ISBN 1-55748-940-8

All rights reserved. No part of this publication may be reproduced or transmitted in any form or by any means without written permission of the publisher.

Published by Barbour & Company, Inc.
P.O. Box 719
Uhrichsville, Ohio 44683
http://www.barbourbooks.com

Member of the
Evangelical Christian
Publishers Association

Printed in the United States of America

Introduction

*"For God so loved the world, that he gave
his only begotten Son, that whosoever
believeth in him should not perish,
but have everlasting life." John 3:16*

*"Beloved, let us love one another: for love is of
God; and every one that loveth is born of God, and
knoweth God. He that loveth not knoweth not
God; for God is love." 1 John 4:7-8*

Many people talk about love, but few people really understand the kind of love about which they speak. Many books have been written about love, but very few people truly understand the kind of love about which they read. God's Word, the Bible, discusses different kinds of love, differences important for us to study and understand. If boys and girls, and men and women, would understand these *Expressions of Love*, their lives would be different. Because these *Expressions of Love* are confused, the already high numbers of teenagers having sex and ultimately producing babies out of wedlock continue to rise: each year, about one million teenage girls get pregnant, and

many of the babies are born illegitimately. Our government spends millions of dollars on inadequate social programs that do not provide enough money to properly feed, clothe, educate, or give the proper medical attention to these babies, then proposes that yet more money allocated for these programs is the solution. Instead of truly helping these teenage girls, the social programs hinder and hurt them. Young people need to know how to discern the particular *Expressions of Love*.

If the various *Expressions of Love* were understood, the divorce rate in the United States would descend from its record-breaking high: one of every three marriages ends up in the divorce courts. Divorce, although touted as the solution to troubled marriages, creates its own mire. Regardless of one's age, comprehending the *Expressions of Love* is essential.

Reader, let's study these *Expressions of Love* so we can learn and grow together. Our handbook for life, the Bible, will show us how God has distinguished these *Expressions of Love*. May I suggest that when you are seeking to gain a deeper understanding of the Word of God, study aids are invaluable, e.g., *W. E. Vine's Expository*

Dictionary, Young's Analytical Concordance to the Bible, a Greek lexicon dictionary, or a Bible with extensive footnotes. Any money spent on Bible study aids is an investment in your spiritual growth and development.

Agape Love
God's Kind of Love

Agape love is the highest expression of love one can experience because it is God's kind of love. In its most basic demonstration, agape love allows us to love our fellowman in spite of everything we dislike about him. It has nothing to do with a person's appearance, behavior, family name, financial status, ability, or race. Agape love does not say, "I will love him if he is nice to me," or "I will love her if she does something for me." No, no! Agape love is unconditional.

John 3:16 states, "For God so loved the world, that he gave his only begotten Son, that whosoever believeth in him should not perish, but have everlasting life." (In the King James

Version of the Bible, words that end in *-eth* mean that the action is a continuous process, all the time.) To be sure we understand what the Spirit of God is saying, let's pull some of the words out of this verse for a closer look.

The word *world* includes everybody—red folks, brown folks, yellow folks, black folks, white folks, plumbers, electricians, ministers, doctors, lawyers, musicians, teachers, chefs, babies, children, teenagers, adults, rich, poor, dope dealers, dope users, gang members, prostitutes, homosexuals, lesbians, thieves, murderers, the homeless, child molesters, and everyone else we can think of. All these people together make up the world for whom God sent His only begotten son to die.

Another word to consider is *gave*, a word I call love in action, because it truly expresses love. Love gives of itself rather than taking for itself. Love can only be known by the action it prompts. A husband who causes trouble for his wife is not showing love toward her. A wife who does not provide a haven for her husband to come home to is not demonstrating love. Parents who neglect to provide instructions, discipline, direction, or correction to their children are not truly loving parents. Reader, when we dedicate

ourselves to doing what is right and best for another person, whatever actions that may involve, we are giving ourselves, and giving is love in action.

The next word is *believeth*. God does not require us to have witnessed His son being given to save the world. He simply said we are to believe it, to have faith in it, and then enjoy the everlasting life that is offered in that verse. Perhaps you think, "I can't understand believing, or faith." Amazingly, we believe a lot of things that we don't understand. Let me ask you a couple of questions: Do you understand how your brain works? Of course not! Question number two: Does that stop you from using your brain? Of course not, again! God said we are to believe on His only begotten son; that is faith in action.

The last word to specifically consider is *whosoever*, and that includes absolutely anyone and everyone. "Whosoever" includes you! It includes me!

Love One Another

Let's reflect on some scriptures that give us a commandment to love one another unconditionally as well as reveal some characteristics of agape love. John 13:34-35 reads, "A new commandment I give unto you, That ye love one another; as I have loved you, that ye also love one another. By this *love* shall all men know that ye are my disciples, if ye have love one to another." (Allow me to make a suggestion here. When you read your Bible, God is talking to you, so make your Bible personal to you. Don't read your Bible and judge someone else; read, and judge yourself, i.e., "A new commandment Jesus gives unto me, that I love others; as Jesus has loved me, that I also love others. By this *love* shall all men know that I am His disciple, if I have love to others.")

If we are going to be disciples of Jesus Christ, we have a choice to make. "If we have love to others" is the qualifying condition in the agreement. We must love others in spite of the wrong they have done to us. When our Lord and Savior was falsely accused, lashed thirty-nine times on His back, and spit on, had His beard plucked out and thorns pressed into His head,

was nailed to the cross and pierced in His side with a spear, how did He respond? After all of that, He prayed, "Father, forgive them; for they know not what they do" (Luke 23:34). So what are our excuses not to love others? We have never had to face this horrible way to die. Therefore, we must forgive our mothers, fathers, brothers, sisters, uncles, aunts, husbands, wives, friends, coworkers, enemies—whoever has done us wrong or talked about us wrongfully. Then, not only must we forgive them, we must also love them.

Remember, people are looking for proof to substantiate our testimony of being followers of Jesus Christ. One criterion is obvious love for others.

Keep God's Commandments

Yet another criterion, established by Jesus Himself, certifies that we are His disciples. Ponder the words of Jesus in John 14:21-24: "He that hath my commandments (or sayings, or

words), and keepeth (or obeys) them, he it is that loveth me: and he that loveth me shall be loved of my Father, and I will love him, and will manifest (or show openly) myself to him. Judas saith unto him, not Iscariot, Lord, how is it that thou wilt manifest thyself unto us, and not unto the world? Jesus answered and said unto him, If a man love me, he will keep (or obey) my words: and my Father will love him, and we will come unto him, and make our abode with him. He that loveth me not keepeth (or obeys) not my sayings: and the word which ye hear is not mine, but the Father's which sent me."

These scriptures are too important for us to hurry by them. We need to carefully dissect them so that we can gain the maximum amount of revelation from them. In verse 21 are two important verbs, or action words, *keepeth* and *loveth*. These words indicate two interdependent actions that we must do, and continue doing, all the time. For example, when we stop keeping the commandments of God, we stop loving Him. Or, when we stop loving Him, we stop keeping His commandments. When we continually keep (or obey) His commandments (or sayings, or words), we continually love Him.

Moving on to verse 23, the word *abode* means a permanent residence. Notice that the words *we* and *our* are plural, referring to the triune Godhead, or Trinity—God the Father, God the Son, and God the Holy Spirit. Jesus promises that the Trinity will take up permanent residence in His disciples. Subsequently, the Holy Spirit will shine in, out from, and through us until everyone around us will know we are different from the world.

Finally, in verse 24, Jesus plainly said if we are not loving Him then we are not keeping (or doing, or obeying) His commandments (or words, or sayings). Our actions attest our love for God.

We can see from the verses we are discussing that agape love does not involve emotions or feelings. Agape love is a decision, an act of the will. If we are doing what He commanded us to do, then we are loving Him; if we are not doing what He commanded, then we are not loving Him. You may be thinking, "But, you don't know what someone has done to me." Jesus, however, made no exceptions. His commandment is unequivocally that we love others even as God is loving us.

Continuing with what John wrote about agape love, let's study several verses from John

15. We are given our standard for loving in verse 12, "This is my commandment, That ye love one another, as I have loved you." How has God loved us? Unconditionally. Selflessly. Sacrificially. Joyfully.

Verse 13 describes the greatest expression of love that has been shown to mankind: "Greater love hath no man than this, that a man lay down his life for his friends." What kind of love would cause one to surrender his choices, desires, ambitions, needs—yes, even his own life—for his friends? Agape love.

Jesus straightforwardly declares the requirement for being His friend in verse 14: "Ye are my friends, if ye do whatsoever I command you." Do you consider yourself to be His friend? Are you obeying Him? If so, then praise God for the friendship of Christ. If not, you are not His friend, but you can be! Ask Him to forgive you for not obeying Him, then dedicate your life to obeying His words.

Jumping to verse 17, Jesus said: "These things I command you, that ye love one another." Apparently God wanted to convince us that we are to love others. For curiosity's sake, count how many times we have already seen the specific

commandment to love one another—I count four times: two times in chapter 13 and two times in chapter 15. And that is only within these two chapters!

In 1 John 3:23, we find this same commandment again. "And this is his commandment, That we should believe on the name of his Son Jesus Christ, and love one another, as he gave us commandment." Let's contemplate 1 John 4:7-8: "Beloved, let us love one another: for love is of God; and every one that loveth is born of God, and knoweth God. He that loveth not knoweth not God; for God is love." God is love, and His agape love was given to us at the new birth (the point of salvation), but we need to develop that love. How? By studying and meditating on agape love. May I suggest that you take some time to read 1 John and count how many times you see the words *love*, *loved*, and *loveth* in this short epistle. God has made some very pointed statements about agape love.

Even after this brief discussion of agape love, we can already understand why our world is so askew. Instead of being awash in agape love, it is brimming with hate and prejudice: white folks don't like black folks, yellow folks don't like red

folks, brown folks don't like white folks, and to top it all off, lighter-skinned black folks don't like darker-skinned black folks. The plain and forthright commandment, however, is to love one another. Obviously, God knew the hearts of mankind, because over and over He patiently emphasizes that we are to love one another. (How many times did we find that commandment?) No one made themselves; we all came from the hands of God, the Creator. If we don't like the color of a person, we should not take our feelings out on that person—his color is beyond his control. We ought to take it up with the One who made all the colors of mankind, confess and seek forgiveness for our hatefulness, and ask Him to fill our hearts to overflowing with His kind of love. Agape love.

Forgive One Another

Let us look at some verses of scripture that explain how agape love works in the area of forgiveness. In Matthew 6:12, Jesus taught His

disciples to pray, "And forgive us our debts, as we forgive our debtors." Let me comment on this verse. Sometimes people have owed me money for years. When, from all appearances, I thought they were never going to pay the debt they owed me, I forgave them and forgot all about their debt. Later, in some instances, they came and paid me. Often people have good intentions of paying money back, but they don't have it at the time. If they don't have it to pay, forgive them of that debt. You may respond, "Wait a minute! They owe me a lot of money." Have you thought about the debt we once owed to God? Except for His mercy, grace, and love, we would be in hell now, paying our debt for our sin. Thank God for sending His only son to die for us, to pay sin's debt for us.

Romans 5:8 describes agape love as it relates to forgiveness, "But God commendeth (or recommends as worthy of trust or attention) his love toward us, in that, while we were yet sinners, Christ died for us." Nothing we did evoked love from God. He forgave because He loved us. He loved us because He is love itself.

Let's return to Matthew 6, this time looking at verses 14 and 15, "For if ye forgive men their

trespasses, your heavenly Father will also forgive you: But if ye forgive not men their trespasses, neither will your Father forgive your trespasses." Notice the point the Lord emphasizes in these verses. The process of forgiving works in a circle. How we forgive the people who wrong us determines how God will forgive us for our wrongdoing. Forgiveness is so important because it affects us on all levels of relationship—the fellowship that we have with our heavenly Father, with other members of the family of God, and with each person we encounter from day to day.

Are you saying, "You just don't know what someone has done to me! They said awful things about me"? So what! If what they said is not true, stop being upset; if what they said is true, make amends as you should. What they said is not important, but forgiving them is.

Mark 11:25-26 admonishes, "And when ye stand praying, forgive, if ye have ought (anything whatever, i.e., a grievance) against any: that your Father also which is in heaven may forgive you your trespasses. But if ye do not forgive, neither will your Father which is in heaven forgive your trespasses." What message is the Holy Spirit trying to communicate to us in these verses? Praying

is a significant part of being Jesus' disciples, but if we are holding a grievance against anybody, our prayers will be hindered. If our prayers are not getting results, we need to examine our hearts, or spirits, for any unforgiving attitude that may be lodged there. Forgiving is not a suggestion; it is a commandment, just like loving one another. Reader, if you have an unforgiving attitude in your heart, confess it to God and pray that He will enable you to overcome it now.

Judge Not

Luke 6:37 admonishes, "Judge not, and ye (or you) shall not be judged: condemn not, and ye shall not be condemned: forgive, and ye shall be forgiven." This verse is one that we need to memorize, because we are quick to condemn and judge. The Lord said judgment is His, and rather than condemn another person, we need to pray for him to see the light of God's truth. One word we should pay particular attention to is the word *shall*, which indicates future tense. We forgive

first and then we are forgiven.

And how many times are we to forgive? Luke 17:3-4 yields the answer: "Take heed to yourselves: If thy brother trespass against thee, rebuke him; and if he repent, forgive him. And if he trespass against thee seven times in a day, and seven times in a day turn again to thee, saying, I repent; thou shalt forgive him." (The word *rebuke* means to tell him of his wrongdoing.)

Let's get Matthew's perspective. "Then came Peter to him, and said, Lord, how oft shall my brother sin against me, and I forgive him? till seven times? Jesus saith unto him, I say not unto thee, Until seven times: but, Until seventy times seven" (Matthew 18:21-22).

Jesus said we are to forgive our fellowman seventy times seven, which works out to be 490 times a day. A week's worth of forgiveness would be 490 times seven, which translates into 3,430 times a week. In a month we would forgive 490 times 31 days which calculates to 15,190 instances. His point ought to be apparent to us. Are we convinced that we are to forgive others for whatever wrong they have done to us?

In Ephesians 4:32, Paul also instructs us to forgive one another: "And be ye kind one to

another, tenderhearted, forgiving one another, even as God for Christ's sake hath forgiven you." The foundation of forgiveness is Jesus Christ. He is the one that is responsible for God forgiving us.

Phileo Love
Friendship, or Brotherly, Love

Phileo love refers to the love of a friendship. While perusing several scriptures, we will realize that phileo and agape love work together. (Eventually we will see that all the expressions of love tie in together.) Proverbs 17:17 proposes, "A friend loveth at all times, and a brother is born for adversity." A true friend will always love, demonstrating that love by sticking with us through thick and thin, or through good and bad. All too often people will be our friends when things are going well for us, but when we are confronted with adverse situations, they are nowhere to be found. Truthfully, they are not friends.

This maxim is posed in Proverbs 18:24: "A man that hath friends must shew himself friendly: and there is a friend that sticketh closer than a brother." The law of friendship has a common principle with the law of forgiveness: the first move is on us. If we are genuine friends to others, others will become genuine friends for us, and they will stick with us closer than our own siblings will. Many families lack closeness because the individual members are not genuine friends—they will hurt, and even kill, one another. Praise God for genuine friends, both within our families and without.

The New Testament contains further verses about phileo love. A couple of verses in the Gospel of John enumerate some personal friends of Jesus among the throngs that followed Him. John 11:5 reveals, "Now Jesus loved Martha, and her sister, and Lazarus." This love is first agape and then phileo—you remember I said that you would see these different expressions of love working together. No particular feelings or emotions are involved here. But move down to verse 36, "Then said the Jews, Behold how he loved him!" Jesus and Lazarus were phileo friends too.

John 15:15 divulges Jesus' friendship with His disciples. "Henceforth I call you not servants; for the servant knoweth not what his lord doeth: but I have called you friends; for all things that I have heard of my Father I have made known unto you." Not only had He taught His disciples; these were men with whom He had walked, eaten, slept, prayed, and traveled for three and one half years. He loved them as if they were His very own brothers, a consummate example of agape love and phileo love working hand in hand.

We already discussed John 15:13-14 in relationship to agape love. Now we see, however, agape love can blend with phileo love. "Greater love hath no man than this, that a man lay down his life for his friends. Ye (or you) are my friends, if ye do whatsoever I command you." In both of these verses Jesus used the word *friends*, meaning a genuine friend. What a perfect picture of the meaning of friend was Jesus Christ Himself when He gave His life so that we could enjoy everlasting life. He willingly became sin for us so we could be free from both sin and the consequences of sin: sickness, disease, poverty, fear, worry, anger, and every bad thing of which we can think.

Permit me to further explain that concept with a practical illustration. What Jesus did for us is similar to if I were to approach one of the boys in jail that I teach and say to him, "Son, you take my clothes and the keys to my car. You're free now; I will serve the rest of your time." That's exactly what Jesus did. He pardoned us from the time we should have served in the prison of hell and took our sentence on Himself.

As we look across our nation, we must conclude that very little phileo love has been taught to our citizens. Schisms have fractured homes, churches, schools, places of employment, housing developments, towns, and cities. Many people haven't a clue as to what brotherly love is all about. Men and women are selling rock cocaine, pills, marijuana, and now ice and every kind of drug to our children and to one another for no other love but the love of money—which is not love at all; it is death. The phileo love our nation needs is characterized in Romans 12:9-10: "Let love be without dissimulation. Abhor that which is evil; cleave to that which is good. Be kindly affectioned one to another with brotherly love; in honour preferring one another."

We need to extract a few words so we can

benefit more fully from what the Holy Spirit is saying to us. The word *let* indicates we have a choice in the matter: will we, or will we not, permit our love to be tainted with dissimulation? God is a perfect gentleman in every aspect and will not override our will or choice to do anything. What He will do, if we will allow Him the opportunity, is influence us to do the right thing in every situation of life. The choice is ours.

The word *dissimulate* means to disguise under a mask. Brotherly love does not deceive, concealing feelings, intentions, and ulterior motives; rather, it is genuine, real, sincere, and transparent.

Another word to particularly notice here is *brotherly*, meaning characteristic of, or befitting, brothers. We must be careful that our definition of "brotherly" is determined by the relationship that God intended should be between brothers, not necessarily the relationships that we may have with our brothers or that we may observe between other brothers.

The last scripture we will look at relating to phileo love is Hebrews 13:1, "Let brotherly love continue." The word *let* again indicates that we have a choice, a decision, and that decision, set

forth by the Biblical writer, concerns the perpetuity of brotherly love. *Continue* never stops. Phileo love should not fluctuate depending on feelings or circumstances. No, no. It ought to go on and on and on and on.

Storge Love
Affectionate Love

Storge love means affectionate love, a love most often displayed to children and elderly people. If storge love were prevalent in our society today, children would receive plenty of properly affectionate pats, caresses, hugs, and kisses. Yet many children today are molested, even by their own parents, siblings, or other relatives. Elderly people would be respected by passersby and respectfully loved by those that care for them, whether the caregivers were related to them or not. The aged would not be, as many of them often are today, neglected and mistreated in hospitals, convalescent homes and rest homes, and their own homes.

God moved through affectionate love to save the life of the infant Moses. Exodus 2:5-6 tells the account: "And the daughter of Pharaoh came down to wash herself at the river;. . .and when she saw the ark among the flags, she sent her maid to fetch it. And when she had opened it, she saw the child: and, behold, the babe wept. And she had compassion on him, and said, This is one of the Hebrews' children." We can almost hear the Pharaoh's daughter's whispery coo, "Aaaaaw!"

Storge love may also be illustrated through the relationship of Hannah with her son Samuel. Although the agape love Hannah nurtured in her heart toward God moved her to vow that should God bless her with a son she would lend him to the Lord "all the days of his life," the storge love she fostered toward Samuel was evident in the "little coat" she brought to him "from year to year, when she came up with her husband to offer the yearly sacrifice" (1 Samuel 1:11, 2:19).

Affectionate love is not reserved solely for the very young and very old. Notice the affection that developed in another Old Testament family. Granted, the affection led to favoritism that culminated in severe circumstances, yet the love

expressed was storge love. "And the boys grew: and Esau was a cunning hunter, a man of the field; and Jacob was a plain man, dwelling in tents. And Isaac loved Esau, because he did eat of his venison: but Rebekah loved Jacob" (Genesis 25:27-28).

The New Testament presents a beautiful picture of storge love in Mark 10:13-16. "And they [the people] brought young children to him [Jesus,] that he should touch them: and his disciples rebuked those that brought them. But when Jesus saw it, he was much displeased, and said unto them, Suffer the little children to come unto me, and forbid them not: for of such is the kingdom of God. Verily I say unto you, Whosoever shall not receive the kingdom of God as a little child, he shall not enter therein. And he took them up in his arms, put his hands upon them, and blessed them." Storge love prompts the tender cradling of a tiny foot, the soft caress of a cherubic dimple, the gentle cuddling of a dreaming toddler.

Now let's move on to the last of the four types of love.

Eros Love
Sexual Love

Eros love means sexual attraction or sexual love. (From the Greek word *eros*, we derive the word *erotic*.) Eros love relates to the other loves like a building relates to its foundation. Agape love, phileo love, and storge love create a solid base for eros love. In this way the loves team up to work together.

Whether within or without marriage, many people today are trying to establish stable relationships on eros love alone, and are dumbfounded when the relationships collapse. Even though the only right setting for eros love is within a marriage, merely validating eros love with a marriage ceremony will not substantiate a strong relationship. Although physical consummation of a marriage does not require the presence of agape, phileo, and storge loves between the marriage partners, the marriage that depends on eros love is tenuous at best. Overwhelming desire to have intercourse with a person will never compensate for lack of commitment.

God is not anti-sex. He knows that sex has a strong hold on both women and men. He

specifically planned for sex to occur, and just as specifically designed for it to be enjoyable, but He also established that the sole rightful context for sex is marriage. And the context means everything.

Let's consider several Old Testament accounts that disclose the nature of eros love. The first example shows eros love out of its rightful place; the second focuses on undisciplined, inordinate eros love, although it is expressed within marriage; and the third showcases proper eros love.

"And Dinah the daughter of Leah, which she bare unto Jacob, went out to see the daughters of the land. And when Shechem the son of Hamor the Hivite, prince of the country, saw her, he took her, and lay with her, and defiled her. And his soul clave unto Dinah the daughter of Jacob, and he loved the damsel, and spake kindly unto the damsel. And Shechem spake unto his father Hamor, saying, Get me this damsel to wife. And Jacob heard that he had defiled Dinah his daughter: now his sons were with his cattle in the field: and Jacob held his peace until they were come" (Genesis 34:1-5).

Shechem not only lusted for Dinah, he also committed fornication with her, a blatant

violation of the law. Although eventually the two were married, Shechem had already defiled Dinah, had already made her morally filthy or unclean. Dinah's brothers were grieved and angry. Genesis 34:25-29 tells of the deceitful and vicious plan they laid and executed to wreak their vengeance on Shechem and his father for the terrible wrong done to their sister: ". . .Dinah's brethren took each man his sword, and came upon the city boldly, and slew all the males. And they slew Hamor and Shechem his son with the edge of the sword, and took Dinah out of Shechem's house, and went out. The sons of Jacob came upon the slain, and spoiled the city, because they had defiled their sister. They took their sheep, and their oxen, and their asses (donkeys), and that which was in the city, and that which was in the field, And all their wealth, and all their little ones, and their wives took they captive, and spoiled even all that was in the house."

1 Kings 11:1 cites the classic example of a man inappropriately overcome with eros love: "But King Solomon loved many strange women, together with the daughter of Pharaoh, women of the Moabites, Ammonites, Edomites, Zidonians, and Hittites." Verse three of the same

chapter verifies that King Solomon "had seven hundred wives, princesses, and three hundred concubines. . ." He lusted for these women with eros love. Most of these women were political pawns in an era when women were treated as chattel and had no choice about what was happening to them, but women have been fooled about the expressions of love down through the centuries. When a man tells a woman he loves her, he often is talking about sexual love, eros love, the only love he has been taught. He often doesn't know anything about agape love. When the woman hears the word love, she often interprets it as a higher love than sexual love, and ends up being violated.

Now let's contrast these first two references with eros love in its proper setting.

When famine struck the land of Israel, Elimelech moved his wife, Naomi, and two sons to the land of Moab. While the family lived there, the sons married—Chilion married Orpah; Mahlon, Ruth. Although the Bible does not disclose the details, all three of the men died. Naomi decided to return to Israel, the famine being ended, but she encouraged her daughters-in-law to stay in Moab to find other husbands

and, hopefully, to raise families. Orpah agreed to the idea, but Ruth had apparently seen something in Naomi that convinced her she would rather be a widow with Naomi than a wife and mother away from her. Ruth's plea to Naomi has become a classic expression of love: "And Ruth said, Intreat me not to leave thee, or to return from following after thee: for whither thou goest, I will go; and where thou lodgest, I will lodge: thy people shall be my people, and thy God my God: Where thou diest, will I die, and there will I be buried: the LORD do so to me, and more also, if ought but death part thee and me" (Ruth 1:16-17).

Naomi conceded.

Because Naomi and Ruth were rather poor, Ruth gathered grain that had fallen behind the field hands, a practice known as gleaning. Unknowingly, but providentially, Ruth gleaned in the fields of Boaz, a relative of Naomi's. When Boaz noticed the new woman among the needy people, he inquired about her. Upon discovering that she was the daughter-in-law of Naomi, of whose virtue he had already heard, Boaz invited her to glean only in his fields and eat with his workers. Unbeknownst to Ruth, he instructed his

hands to purposely let extra grain fall for her.

Boaz was older than Ruth and apparently somewhat shy, explaining, perhaps, why he had not married already, but Naomi was nobody's dummy. When she saw what was happening, she set out to do some matchmaking. Naomi coached Ruth in the marriage customs and laws of Israel, and Ruth carefully followed each suggestion.

By the end of the harvest time, Boaz had come to love Ruth. He approached the men of authority in the city to seek permission to marry Ruth. When all the legal matters involved were resolved, with the blessing of the people—including Naomi, Boaz made Ruth his wife. (Read the entire story for yourself; this summary skips too many details!)

The progression through the expressions of love is heart-warming. Agape love welcomed Ruth to glean in Boaz' fields even though legally he could have denied her access because she was a foreigner. Phileo love surfaced as he not only allowed her the gleanings, but promised her protection and fed her from his table. The verbalization of Boaz' storge love surely elicited smiles from his hired hands as he directed them to drop extra grain specifically for Ruth to gather. With

the groundwork laid and the legal issues settled, eros love completed their relationship.

Reader, I do not mean to sound arrogant as I present this discourse on the expressions of love. I have not always had the information or knowledge that I am sharing with you now. I have messed up also, but I want to provoke you to think. Sir, if you tell a girl or woman you want to have sex with her because you love her, you are telling an untruth. Ma'am, if a boy or man says he wants to have sex with you because he loves you, he is lying. If you truly love someone, you do not behave immorally with him or her, nor do you take for yourself what does not belong to you. When, or if, you are of marriageable age, you will first commit yourselves to each other in marriage, and only afterwards enjoy a sexual relationship together.

I am not denying the desire to have sex with someone you love. The desire is there—God created us as sexual beings, fully intending for us to find pleasure in sex within marriage, but God can empower us to live pure lives. I can testify from personal experience of His power to live a pure life—my wife and I never had sex before we were married—and His power is available to you too.

Acknowledging sexual desire and succumbing to it (outside of marriage), however, are two very different issues. Commitment to agape love will enable us to maintain righteous relationships because agape love transcends sexual desire, emotions, and feelings. Agape love puts sexual desire, emotions, and feelings in their proper perspectives and places.

Husbands, Love Your Wives

Several scriptures command husbands to love their wives. The media has influenced us to think so disproportionately about eros love in marriage that the other loves are all but ignored. Several verses in Ephesians 5 set the order for the love between husbands and wives. Verse 25 commands agape love, "Husbands, love your wives, even as Christ also loved the church and gave himself for it." Let me pull out a few important points about this verse. Agape love is dependent on the will, not the emotions. Did Christ eagerly choose to love the church to the point of

death? No. Matthew 26:39 reveals His struggle in making that choice. "And he went a little farther, and fell on his face, and prayed, saying, O my Father, if it be possible, let this cup pass from me: nevertheless not as I will, but as thou wilt." But He made the choice, a decision of His will, to submit to the will of the Father for the salvation of the church. Christ gave His very life, the ultimate expression of agape love.

We complain, "But she makes me so angry! She can't do this, and she won't do that." How petty! What do our feelings have to do with extending agape love to our wives? We are to make a choice, a decision, to love our wives unconditionally.

Our love is not to be mechanical, however. Expressions of love should come naturally. Look at Ephesians 5:28, "So ought men to love their wives as their own bodies. He that loveth his wife loveth himself." Just how much thought do we actually give before deciding to care for our own bodies? Very little. The decision is either nearly automatic or a matter of course. We smash our thumbs with a hammer, and instantly grab that throbbing thumb and care for it. We come home bone-tired from a hard day's work, plop down on

the couch or recliner, and prop up our feet. When we are hungry, we rummage in the cupboard or fridge, call for a pizza, or look for the nearest restaurant. We find some way to satisfy our rumbling stomachs. Nighttime comes and we give our bodies rest. We pillow our heads on downy pillows and snuggle under a warm blanket. Are you saying, "Of course!"? Then I have made my point. Our love for our wives should find expression that naturally.

To watch the way some men treat their wives, we would have to conclude they must not love themselves very much at all. A record produced many years ago sported the title, "Love Is a Hurting Thing." I was not a Christian at that time, but I knew I wanted nothing to do with a hurting love. True love never hurts; it only gives and gives and gives of itself. Sir, if you are hurting your wife, you are not loving her.

Oftentimes men and women have married without ever understanding agape love because they rushed into their relationship at the level of eros love, sexual attraction, before they had laid the necessary groundwork of agape love. They began talking because he thought she was beautiful, cute, and funny, and she thought he was a

knockout or saw that he drove a nice car or noticed that he was a sharp dresser. Perhaps he was voted student council president or the most valuable player on the team, or she was a cheerleader or homecoming queen. Or perhaps they were "nobodies" who made each other feel like "somebody." Whatever the situation, they enjoyed each other's company and found pleasure simply in being together.

Next, storge love, or affection, and phileo love, or friendship love, entered the picture. They began to hold hands, then progressed to quick hugs and little kisses on the cheek. He purchased little gifts—candy or cards or flowers—for her and did little favors that made her feel loved. She admired his strength and chivalry. The development of the storge and phileo loves coupled with the initial eros love convinced the couple that they had all the components of a solid relationship, though they—unknowingly or not—neglected the bedrock of agape love.

Gradually, they changed to kissing on the lips and hugging longer and more tightly. In time, the heat of passion overruled their consciences, and they involved themselves in immorality. The devil may have told them sex

with each other was all right because they loved each other so much, because they had such a strong relationship. (He *will* lie to us; no truth is in him.) A physical relationship that disdains the prerequisite of marriage and bypasses agape love is not right.

Understandably, although wrongfully, many single teenage girls get pregnant. Obviously, these girls do not become pregnant by themselves—our young men are at fault as well. Many fellows simply evade the consequences of their behavior. No one has taught them how to love with agape love.

The same lack of knowledge is responsible for the record-breaking number of marriages ending in the divorce courts. Marriages based on eros love rather than agape love are unstable from the very start, and because they are faulty from the beginning, tremendous energy and effort must be expended to turn them around. Let me make one more comment on marriage. Many marriages could be rescued if the couple would not give up so easily. Marriage is a faith fight all the way.

Regrettably, our nation is suffering the effects of premarital and extramarital sex. Today

many couples are living together, justifying the situation by saying that their relationship is based on love, but it is eros love, which is sexual attraction. The reason they are living together is that they have been taught to live together, and that teaching came from permissiveness and/or observation.

A common proverb states that for evil to prevail good men need to do nothing. Parents who either silently agreed or only weakly resisted as their children deviated from biblical injunctions regarding sex contributed horrifically to the ensuing blatant promiscuity in our country. Pastors and evangelists who neglected to emphasize holiness and purity in every area of our lives actually assisted in the results rampant today. We need continuous renewing of our minds by the Word of God if we are to measure up to the spiritual standard God requires. When we let down our guard, we soon let down our standard.

All too often, however, these couples living together first observed the practice as individuals growing up in their own homes as they were growing up. Let me give you a good example: A woman who is living alone meets a man and invites him over to her home or apartment for

dinner. He ends up spending the night with her. The following week he visits her home and ends up spending another night there. In no time at all, the man has moved in, and the couple is living together permanently. (This situation could be reversed, i.e., a woman moving in with a man, but I see it happening more often the other way around.) Here is the point: many of these women have little children who see the man living there and conclude that his living with them is not wrong. Those women have taught their children by her example; they have been taught by observation. In my own family, I saw my mother let her boyfriend move into our home, and tragically, my sisters followed that same example. That is what they were taught by observation. Living carefully and righteously is so important; somewhere, people are always watching us. A common statement says, "What you do speaks so loud I can't hear what you say." Let's live our lives in obedience to God, and let our children observe a right (righteous) example.

Without being obnoxious or demeaning, be alert to learn the family history of a woman who has become pregnant out of wedlock. In most cases, immorality has been in the family for two,

three, or perhaps even four generations. This curse upon the family has to be broken. Christ was made a curse for us so that we can be set free from the curse of the law (Galatians 3:13).

This principle also applies to a curse in many families with teenage boys going to jail. I teach at an institution for boys who have been locked up for breaking the law. When I have asked the boys to raise their hands if they have a family member who has been to jail, nine out of ten boys raise their hands. This curse has affected my own family. I was in jail at an early age. When I asked my father and grandfather about family members who had been in jail, I found out that not only had they served time in jail, but my brother had too. The curses of sin have a tenacious grip on these families, but that grip can be broken. I know that because, praise God, I am a free man today. By His grace, I will never go back to jail again except to teach God's Word there. Jesus has the power and grace to enable His disciples—us—to break free from Satan's cursed grip and live holy, righteous lives.

Talk and Walk

We've tracked several problems down to a possible cause: misunderstanding the expressions of love. But what's behind the misunderstanding? Perhaps the answer can be found in Titus 2:3-5, "The aged women likewise, that they be in behaviour as becometh holiness, not false accusers, not given to much wine, teachers of good things; That they may teach the young women to be sober, to love their husbands, to love their children, To be discreet, chaste, keepers at home, good, obedient to their own husbands, that the word of God be not blasphemed."

This Scripture portion is directed to the aged, or older, women. Their first responsibility to their families and society is to maintain their relationships to God, which will engender holy lives. The word *holiness*, although a noun, involves action. Holiness will not characterize their lives accidentally. They must make moment-by-moment decisions to adhere to a lifestyle entirely devoted, or pleasing, to God. (Men, these thoughts about holiness apply to us too!)

God Himself prescribed that the aged women, or the older women, are to *teach*, both by

word and example, *the young women*. However, unless these women are fulfilling their first responsibility, i.e., their relationships to God, they are not qualified for, nor can they perform properly, their role as teachers. Admittedly, some older women did not have a godly example lived before them, or if they had the example they did not pass that example down from the generation from which they got it, but the obligation to live holy lives remains. One's relationship with God is an individual issue, and any woman can begin and develop a personal walk with God. (Again, men, these passages apply to us too!)

Not much teaching is happening between older women and younger women and older men and younger men today. The devastating outcome is that many younger men and women are not loving their wives and husbands as they ought to love them, and troubled marriages, separations, and divorces plague our nation's homes.

Nor are many children being loved as they ought to be. I make that statement because the numbers are growing at the correctional school for boys at which I teach. More boys are coming in than we have facilities to house. I heard a report that more than 8,000 boys and girls are

incarcerated in the state of California alone. Think about the other 49 states and the U.S. territories. Even if only 4,000 are detained in the other states, calculate how many juveniles are locked up: more than two hundred thousand. We don't have enough jails and juvenile halls to hold the children.

Children need more than simple teaching about chastity; they must see it exemplified and honored in the lives of the adults around them. The definition of *chaste* (in Titus 2:5) goes beyond innocence of unlawful sexual intercourse, an outward behavior. Chastity requires inward purity in thought and desire as well. Because of the lack of godly teaching about and examples of chastity, the numbers of teenage pregnancies out of wedlock continue to escalate. Particularly in today's government schools, children are taught plenty about sex, but they are taught, yes, even encouraged, to experiment rather than abstain. After parents have pushed God, His Word, and His authority out of their lives and homes, and administrators and legislators have ousted Him from the classroom, the children and young people believe they have no reason to live righteously.

Reader, can you see why we need to be able to distinguish the various *Expressions of Love?* why we ought to learn as much as possible about agape love? why we need to teach our children about agape love at home? why we need to be involved in a church that teaches God's Word and portrays His love without compromising? A wonderful first lesson on agape love for us and our children is straight from the Word of God. Read and study carefully 1 Corinthians chapter 13, often called the love chapter. This portion of scripture describes in practical detail how agape love impacts our everyday lives.

Can you see the importance of developing dependable phileo friendships? of strengthening the ties that bind our families together? of serving a cup of cold water in Jesus' name? of extending the hand of friendship to whomever we can possibly befriend? Two good lessons on phileo love come from the life of David. 1 Samuel 20 reveals the strength of his friendship with Jonathan, and 2 Samuel 1 exposes his grief after Jonathan's death. In 2 Samuel 9 David honors his friend's memory by showing kindness to Jonathan's son. Study these chapters together

with your family.

Are you aware of the necessity for proper expressions of storge love? of hugging your children? of tucking them in at night? of smoothing the brow of an elderly person? of holding her hand? of assisting him with chores? of simply taking the time to converse with them? 1 Peter 3:8 and 1 John 3:17, respectively, are perfect discussion starters about storge love. "Finally, be ye all of one mind, having compassion one of another, love as brethren, be pitiful, be courteous." "But whoso hath this world's good, and seeth his brother have need, and shutteth up his bowels of compassion from him, how dwelleth the love of God in him?"

Are you convinced that the disproportionate emphasis on eros love must be adjusted? that eros love must needs be revealed for what it is, and for what it is not? that eros love requires a strong foundation of the other loves? that we must conform to the standard God has established regarding eros love? The four chapters of the Book of Ruth furnish a beautiful and classic specimen of the intertwined expressions of love. Don't miss it!

As I conclude this book about the *Expressions*

of Love, I readily admit that I have not said all there is to say on the subject; neither have I disclosed all of the scriptures about the four kinds of love. If you will build on the foundation you have laid with this brief discourse, however, allowing the Holy Spirit to lead you from what we have already learned into an even deeper understanding, your life will be changed to reflect more and more of God's love. Then use your knowledge and understanding to help someone else see the light of God's Word. We are in this faith walk together to grow, to learn how to love one another, and to have an impact on our sin-sick world. Resolve with me to study the Word of God to learn more about the *Expressions of Love,* and then to put that knowledge into practice, loving people the way God loves people.

ONLY 99¢!

What's the greatest thing in the world?

Love. Only love can provide the greatest peace, the greatest happiness, the greatest fulfillment in life. For only love can guide men and women to faith in Jesus Christ, and only God's love can heal our world.

Available wherever books are sold.
Or order from:
Barbour & Company, Inc.
P.O. Box 719
Uhrichsville, Ohio 44683
http://www.barbourbooks.com